The First 100 Days on the Job

How to Plan, Prioritise and Build a Sustainable Organisation

T0298875

Anne Augustine

The Convergency Partnership, hello@convergencypartnership.com

First published in 2012 by Dō Sustainability
87 Lonsdale Road, Oxford OX2 7ET, UK

ISBN 978-1-909293-16-8 (eBook-ePub)
ISBN 978-1-909293-17-5 (eBook-PDF)
ISBN 978-1-909293-15-1 (Paperback)

A catalogue record for this title is available from the British Library.

At Dō Sustainability we strive to minimize our environmental impacts and carbon footprint through reducing waste, recycling and offsetting our CO_2 emissions, including those created through publication of this book. For more information on our environmental policy see **www.dosustainability.com**.

Page design and typesetting by Alison Rayner
Cover by Becky Chilcott

For further information on Dō Sustainability, visit our website:
www.dosustainability.com

DōShorts

Dō Sustainability is the publisher of **DōShorts**: short, high-value ebooks that distil sustainability best practice and business insights for busy, results-driven professionals. Each DōShort can be read in 90 minutes.

New and forthcoming DōShorts -- stay up to date

We publish 3 to 5 new DōShorts each month. The best way to keep up to date? Sign up to our short, monthly newsletter. Go to **www. dosustainability.com/newsletter** to sign up to the Dō Newsletter. Some of our latest and forthcoming titles include:

- *Green Jujitsu: Embed Sustainability into Your Organisation*
  Gareth Kane
- *How to Make your Company a Recognised Sustainability Champion*   Brendan May
- *Making the Most of Standards* Adrian Henriques
- *Promoting Sustainable Behaviour: A Practical Guide to What Works*   Adam Corner
- *Solar Photovoltaics Business Briefing*   David Thorpe
- *Sustainability in the Public Sector*   Sonja Powell
- *Sustainability Reporting for SMEs*   Elaine Cohen
- *Sustainable Transport Fuels Business Briefing*   David Thorpe
- *The Changing Profile of Corporate Climate Change Risk*
  Mark Trexler & Laura Kosloff
- *The First 100 Days: Plan, Prioritise & Build a Sustainable Organisation*   Anne Augustine
- *The Short Guide to SRI*   Cary Krosinsky

Subscriptions

In additional to individual sales and rentals, we offer organisational subscriptions to our full collection of published and forthcoming books. To discuss a subscription for your organisation, email **veruschka@dosustainability.com**

Write for us, or suggest a DōShort

Please visit **www.dosustainability.com** for our full publishing programme. If you don't find what you need, write for us! Or Suggest a DōShort on our website. We look forward to hearing from you.

....

Abstract

ANYONE WHO HAS SPENT TIME in organisations, regardless of size or sector, will know that the demands of any leadership role are contradictory, often conflicting and almost always challenging. It's the landscape of the world of work. But there is a more fundamental shift happening, a shift that is bringing the expectations of the world at large to the doors of organisations that have never acknowledged or responded to these challenges before. That shift is sustainable development and the call for organisations to act in partnership with other businesses, government and civil society – perhaps even taking on a leadership role – in new ways that are not solely based on profit, but on the creation of mutual value. And within those organisations, individuals are driven to respond. If you are one of those people who has been asked, or chose, to lead change for sustainability, then this DōShort is for you.

It offers:

- A process, if you will, to make the most of the first 100 days

- Some tools you can use to manage your programme

- A heavy dose of realism about what can be done, to keep you sane.

In the absence of complete and perfect information you will be expected to lead and to act. It is the *timing* of decision-making rather than the decisions per se that will set you apart. Harvard Business School academics Bob Eccles and Nitin Nohria call this 'robust action',

ABSTRACT

which 'accomplishes short-term objectives while preserving long-term flexibility'. You need to act in parallel with the development of a longer-term strategy, and with large doses of uncertainty, and in the context of an organisation that will be constantly shifting in response to internal and external stimuli. And in the meantime, you need to ensure your first 100 days in the role set you up for that success.

....

About The Author

 **WITH AN INTERNATIONAL** and multi-sector career spanning sustainability leadership, programme management, business development and consulting with global multinationals – including HP/EDS, Microsoft and Edelman – **Anne Augustine** works with organisations in transition.

She is the founder and director of the small and beautifully formed Convergency Partnership (**http://www.convergencypartnership.com**), a consultancy that combines business, academia, science, and the arts, to help create innovative and sustainable change.

Anne has helped global organisations define and implement corporate strategy, she has worked with start up companies to shape their vision, and with established businesses to engage with their stakeholders in more meaningful and transparent ways. She has coached board-level executives and acted as facilitator for grassroots organisations.

She is also a Visiting Business Fellow at the Smith School of Enterprise and the Environment, a multidisciplinary research hub at Oxford University that brings together government, academia and business to collaborate on responding to the challenge of climate change.

Acknowledgements

THERE ARE SO MANY FRIENDS, mentors and colleagues who have helped shape my thinking and doing over the years, and in so many ways their wisdom and impact is reflected in what I have written. Particular thanks go to my reviewers – Dr Marc Ventresca, Ron Smith and Chris Kemp – for their suggestions and feedback, and for helping to fill some of the memory gaps while I wrote this DōShort.

Contents

CONTENTS

Introduction

IN EARLY 2008, after going to nag Electronic Data Systems's (EDS) Vice President of the Europe Middle East & Africa (EMEA) region about the fact that we didn't appear to be doing anything about sustainability, I was told to go and make something happen. No team, no budget, no promotion, but two clear goals: 1) to take cost and environmental impact out of the business operations in the calendar year, and 2) to make sure that sustainability, and my involvement in bids, directly contributed to signing outsourcing deals.

I had to have a bottom-line and a top-line EMEA-wide impact – and within 12 months – with no other resources than me and a 'virtual' team of colleagues from different parts of EDS's business for whom sustainability was another thing they had to factor into their busy lives! I became part of a global team of three whose day job it was to lead Sustainability – one for the Americas (and with global oversight), one for EMEA and one for Asia Pacific. This was for a $27bn business employing around 100,000 employees globally!

I did the job for 18 months before being made redundant as part of Hewlett-Packard's (HP) acquisition of EDS. Did we achieve the grand vision some of us had of transforming EDS into an environmentally responsible and authentically engaged global business? In a word, no. But we did achieve far more than some might have thought possible when going through companywide organisational uncertainty due to acquisition and takeover.

It turned out that colleagues in Procurement and Sales & Marketing in the UK had been working on projects since 2007. The key issues for EDS UK at the time were the rapidly rising cost of electricity and sales teams responding to environment-related Request For Proposal (RFP) questions from major government clients. Building on their early work, and that of colleagues in Australia who were developing a business offering in response to the National Greenhouse and Energy Reporting (NGER) Scheme, we did:

- Develop a global environmental sustainability strategy, signed off by the board.

- Reduce absolute carbon emissions and energy consumption in our UK data centres.

- Complete a comprehensive, auditable, baseline of our environmental impacts.

- Create and sell a consulting offering for clients to develop Green IT strategies.

- Integrate sustainability into a newly signed $1bn outsourcing contract through the development of a Green Service Level Agreement (SLA).

- Create an EMEA wide network of grassroots champions to share information and support each other.

- Establish community engagement groups to work within local areas for fundraising and local projects.

- Participate in International Business Leaders' Forum IT for Africa programme, taking full responsibility for all technology waste management.

- Win an award for the design of a new, energy-efficient data centre, developed in partnership with the Rocky Mountain Institute.

- Raise employee awareness of sustainability through one-to-one discussion, intranet blogs, Twitter and staff newsletters.

- Participate in enterprise level governance initiatives, such as the EU Code of Conduct for Data Centre Energy Efficiency, ISO 14001 certification, Carbon Disclosure Project and the Green Grid's Data Centre Standards.

- Attain high scores for our strategy and results from industry analysts.

There were lots more projects – in fact, there was far more going on than any one person had visibility of. It didn't always feel like part of an integrated strategy, and that the superficial parts were adding up to a substantial whole. Or that we had a clear direction. Or that I was being an effective change leader. It was exhausting and exhilarating. Nothing ever seemed like it was enough. For every organisational supporter there were more suspicious onlookers.

We had to say no to people about things that actually made sense. I would make a commitment to do something only to be told I couldn't. There weren't enough hours in the day, or hands, to keep the plates spinning. Decisions, and resulting action, were delayed or never made because of the acquisition. It was lonely. Especially when I knew my job was on the line. It felt like I was making it up as I went along (guess what, I was) but I would have lost considerable 'face' by asking for help or falling short of delivering a transformation that was 'market making'.

But for all that, those 18 months were the high point of my career to date. I was doing work that had meaning and significance as well as commercial impact. I could see change starting to happen in miniscule ways, opinions shifting, projects approved (or not rejected outright!) and colleagues (sometimes very senior) approaching me rather than me approaching them. And EDS made some industry leading innovations in the face of acquisition and subsequent integration.

We barely scratched the surface of what was necessary, possible and right. But we made the beginnings of an indent. I learned a tremendous amount: about what people are capable of when they believe in what they're doing, how change happens (even more slowly than you think, and not always in the way that you expect), that willpower and charm alone will not shift an organisation if the leadership team doesn't engage with it, and how important it is to have a plan even if you don't stick to it.

Since then, I have been seconded into a one company as their interim sustainability manager, and worked as sustainability strategy consultant for organisations ranging from supermarket retailers to smart city developers, grassroots campaigners and social enterprises in developing markets. I have followed the fortunes and failings of many of our leading brands and businesses.

I hope that this DōShort distils my own experiences, what I have seen with others, what I wish someone had told me, and some research into starting up a sustainability initiative. And that this distillation is useful for you in three ways:

- A process, if you will, to make the most of the first 100 days

- Some tools you can use to manage your programme

- A heavy dose of realism about what can be done, to keep you sane.

There are many things I don't know about you and your context – where you sit in your organisation, your capabilities, personality and leadership style, your sponsor, resources (time, people and money) at your disposal, organisational culture and management, the industry sector and geographic reach, who your stakeholders are and what is driving the nascent sustainability agenda. What I am certain about is that in this transition you don't need to have a job title that includes the words 'sustainability' or 'CSR'.

Malcolm Gladwell, author of *Outliers* (**http://www.gladwell.com/outliers/index.html**), said that it takes 10,000 hours, or 10 years, to attain mastery. No doubt you have mastery – in your industry, organisation and its culture, the formal and informal networks, your professional role – and tacit knowledge. These are experiences and skills to build on as you take the first steps to a new mastery – that of bringing about change for sustainability.

Over the years I have spoken with sustainability champions within organisations of all shapes and sizes. Many of these people believe, as I do, that the ultimate measure of our success as change agents is that our role becomes no longer necessary. That is my aspiration. Organisations no longer see sustainability as something that's 'done' by the PR team, or the IT department or the bean counters in Finance, something that requires a groundswell of mavericks and rebels to make it happen. It becomes part of the fabric of how business is done and led from the top; for the long-term benefit of business *and* society. But we have a lot of work to do before then. And with increasing urgency.

I hope this DōShort gives you some structure to take the foundational steps of this eventful journey into the unknown: *The First 100 Days on the Job: How to Plan, Prioritise and Build a Sustainable Organisation.*

....

A Few Words About You

YOU ARE GOING TO HAVE TO ADJUST very quickly in these first 100 days – learning new skills and applying existing skills in different ways. Fundamentally, knowing how stuff gets done and how to get your stuff done. Dr Marc J. Ventresca, a Fellow at Oxford University who teaches Strategy Implementation, talks about getting clarity on the **'3 Rs' – relationships, resources and rules of the game** (a model he developed in partnership with Dr. William Ocasio from Northwestern University). Top tip – if you take nothing else from this DōShort, remember the '3 Rs' – they will stand you in good stead!

I think there are five key characteristics that you will need to exhibit as change agent in addition to the expertise that has got you where you are today:

- **Influence** – organisations are very resistant to change, even good change

- **Communication** – which means listening as much (if not more than) talking

- **Adaptability** – things will change, most likely outside of your control

- **Innovation** – be entrepreneurial when seeking out how to create value

- **Delivery** – yes, you are going to have to achieve something. And soon. But not too soon.

And critically, for your own well-being, don't try to become someone you're not. Yes, there will be new skills to learn, habits to moderate and assumptions to be challenged, but if you no longer recognise the person who's looking back at you in the mirror it's time to check in on the values and goals that motivated you in the first place. Seriously, you are in this for the long haul, so look after yourself.

....

What Is Sustainability, Anyway?

THE GOAL OF THIS BOOK IS TO HELP YOU accelerate through your first 100 days as a change agent for sustainability. For the most part, I have written this DōShort with the perspective that this is something you have chosen to do, whether or not it came with a new sign on your desk. That said, I know there are far more organisations, and leaders, who know that they need to do something about sustainability but not what (or why, or how). And that someone gets tasked to work it out, quickly. Maybe that someone is you.

The premise of this DōShort is that you are making changes in an organisational, most likely commercial, context. So what does sustainable development mean for you?

Our way of living as connected, mobile and increasingly developed societies is dependent on a supply of inputs (minerals, oil energy, etc.) that are finite and also increasing in demand. At some point, and futurists say at around 2050, when the global population exceeds nine billion, there will not be enough 'input' stuff to satisfy the lifestyle expectations of so many people (at least four billion of whom will be deemed 'middle class'). Economic growth, notions of prosperity and well-being will need to be achieved with fewer resources, and with more effective re-use of these finite inputs. That's going to require bucket loads of innovation, behaviour change and collaboration (between teams, departments, businesses, supply chains, industry sectors and civic stakeholders).

And so, according to SustainAbility, this presents an opportunity for business:

> *While sustainability is about the future of our society, for today's industries and businesses, it is also about commercial success. The mandate to transform businesses to respect environmental limits while fulfilling social wants and needs has become an unparalleled platform for innovation on strategy, design, manufacturing and brand, offering massive opportunities to compete and to adapt to a rapidly evolving world.*

Simply put, sustainability offers your organisation an opportunity to become a responsible business.

As we go through this DōShort, I am viewing sustainability as a journey to responsibility for your business, starting where you are now, and for whatever reason it is that you have decided to act now.

In 2012, UK retailer Marks & Spencer became carbon neutral (**http://plana.marksandspencer.com/about/carbon-neutral/cutting-carbon**), five years after initiating their 'Plan A' sustainability programme. It has taken time and a significant amount of change in their business to achieve this goal. When they first decided to act, it wasn't with the intention of becoming carbon neutral, but because something was driving them to change the way they did business. They had a 'burning platform', some reason that caused them to act, and to act at that particular time. For many organisations, this burning platform is commercially driven, through customer expectation, operating costs, regulatory or legislative pressures.

What is your burning platform?
....

Why 100 Days?

THE ACTIONS YOU TAKE during your first three months in a new role will largely determine whether you succeed or fail, says Michael Watkins author of the *First 90 Days* (**http://www.michaeldwatkins.com/book-90days.php**). The 90–100-day performance phenomenon is a limiting paradox. You are new into the role, it may even be a new role without precedent, and many accept it takes six months to two years to learn a job properly (and, as Gladwell points out, 10 years to attain mastery). If you fail to build momentum, permission and credibility during this phase, you will face an uphill battle from that point forward. There was a compelling reason to act now, and so you are expected to respond with the same degree of urgency, although the direction may seem unclear.

In Hay Group's (a global management consultancy) experience of working with leaders across all sectors and organisational sizes, according to a recent article in *Management Today* (**http://www.managementtoday. co.uk/news/1147175/Becoming-boss-good-impression-first-week/ ?DCMP=ILC-SEARCH**), they find that leaders who make a rapid and effective impact in their role and set the course ahead for smoother waters concentrate on getting two factors right: creating clarity and setting standards.

The First 10 Days

SO HERE IS MY SECOND TOP TIP: start before you start. When the new role officially kicks in, in whatever way that is reflected in your organisation, be prepared with preliminary due diligence under your belt and an approach for what your first three months are going to look like. Think of it like the timeline below:

$$T\text{-}10 \rightarrow 0 \rightarrow 30 \rightarrow 60 \rightarrow 90$$

Use those 10 days before you are effectively in post to do your fact-finding and early networking. The suggested plan below assumes that you are already within the organisation and have access to the people and information you need to undertake your research. If you are new to the organisation, you could use this plan once you have started. It is developed from a model shared by Simon Berry, a leading business coach.

- **Define objectives** – what is it, specifically, that your sponsor(s) wants you to do, i.e. why were you given the role? What are you going to do?

- **Meet & greet** – find out as much as you can about the organisation, find and meet as many stakeholders as time allows, ask questions, listen to responses.

- **Conduct SWOT** – what issues can you see, root causes, opportunities to be leveraged and dots that can be joined; where are the gaps?

- **Clarify approach** – what is your way forward; identify some quick wins, and the resources needed. Do you know everything you need to right now?

- **Recalibrate objectives** – with what you have discovered so far, how are you going to achieve your objectives? How are you going to measure success?

These first 10 days are the opportunity for you to demonstrate your competence, credibility and compatibility, whatever the organisational culture. And, most critically, this is a great time to build relationships, as right now you don't want anything other than to find out what your colleagues and peers need.

Use the outputs and findings from these first 10 days to create your programme plan – the working document that outlines the job at hand, not just for the next 90 days but also into the medium to longer term.

....

The Next 30, 60, 90 Days

THIS SECTION CONTAINS THE SUBSTANTIVE TOOLS and insights to making your first 100 days effective and successful. In writing this DōShort, I kept changing my mind about the sequence or prioritisation of what needs to be done. Was it possible to be so prescriptive? Only you will be the best judge of where to start, because only you know where you are. For what it's worth, I started with the plan. And if nothing else, I would suggest you do too.

The four tools that will set you up to succeed are:

- Have a strategic plan
    a. Define your terms of reference
    b. Too soon for a strategy?
    c. What is material to your organisation?
    d. Don't forget the golf balls
    e. Your 30, 60, 90 day plan

- Re-learn the organisational context
    a. Adopt the beginner's mind
    b. Surveying the landscape
    c. Doesn't everyone feel the same?
    d. Adding value
    e. TIPS

- Achieve something

  a. Deciding on the quick win

  b. Creating an action plan

  c. Brainstorms that buzz

  d. Managing change

  e. Being open to emergent change

- Be resilient and adaptable

  a. Finding meaning through work

  b. What's driving you?

  c. Where are your values?

  d. Adjusting to leadership

  e. Building your support network

About that plan. While there are four key tools, five if you include the first 10 days, the section on planning is by far the most detailed and practical. This is for one simple reason – in my view, thorough planning in these early days underpins everything else that you will want to accomplish. It is the one thing that you want to have completed as your transition phase in the new role comes to an end. That is not to say you need to spend three months in a locked room preparing elegant Gantt charts, nor that you only act on what is in the plan, but critically by going through a planning and consultation cycle you will gain insight into what is the job at hand.

The other tools are ongoing (although planning is an iterative task too) but they need to be initiated during the first 100 days.

And then there is the quick win.

1. **Have a strategic plan**

There is no way to better instil confidence in yourself and with your stakeholders than to have a plan. And you will have multiple plans – your first 10 days, the first three months and then the longer-term implementation plan. They should be complementary and build on each other.

EDS was a data-driven organisation, with its own proprietary management methodologies, including systems for project management and programme control. They were cumbersome, process-heavy and not at all user-friendly (unless the user was equally and methodically process-driven, which I am not). They certainly didn't tell you *how* to manage.

When I was given the role of sustainability lead at EDS I began to work with a whole new set of organisational stakeholders. Time-short, information-hungry, results-focused. Leaders who were interested in the so what, and what was next. But they still expected these documents to exist and for someone else to have read them. It was, after all, part of the organisation's psyche to have a methodology and audit trail.

Your organisation might have a methodology for how this programme should be managed and what the plan looks like. Or maybe you have experience as a project or programme manager. In the first instance, create a document that has a familiar feel to your sponsors and stakeholders, even if you only ever present a subset of the whole.

Define your terms of reference

So, here is my next top tip. It may be expedient to use the processes in place to manage your endeavours. But there is a simpler, and far quicker, approach to strategic planning in remembering the mnemonic 'BOSCARD'. Developed by Cap Gemini as their project management methodology, BOSCARD is now a freely and widely used way of developing terms of reference for projects and programmes:

Background	• What was the rationale or need for creating this project?
	• What are the anticipated outcomes and benefits?
	• Who are the primary and secondary stakeholders?
Objectives	• What are the specific, measurable, achievable, realistic and timely objectives that drive this project forward?
Scope	• What are the changes, features or outputs that this project will deliver?
	• What are the work streams of activity that need to be done?
	• What, specifically, is out of scope?
Constraints	• What restrictions exist that will have an impact on the scope?
	• What other limiting factors may affect the project?
Assumptions	• What do you currently assume to be true that might have a positive or negative impact, and that need validation?
Resources	• What do you need in the way of time, money and people to implement this project?
	• How are you going to track this for reporting purposes?

Deliverables	• What must the project deliver in order to achieve the objectives?
	• How is the project to be implemented?
	• By what means will you know the project is complete?

You will be judged not only on the quality of your strategy, but more likely on your ability to implement it and get the job done. Well-defined terms of reference and a supporting plan demonstrates that you know the job at hand, what's required to deliver and what success looks like. It will also become a key communication tool. And sometimes a stick when carrots don't work! BOSCARD is the clearest way I know to create a rounded and credible plan, and I still use it as a checklist when I start something new.

Too soon for a strategy?

Having a plan is not the same as having a strategy however. For me, a strategy is about having an idea of where you are going, why you are going in that direction, and how you will get there (and how you will *know* when you get there). The plan helps you execute that strategy by breaking it down into phases of activity so that you can track progress against the goals and manage expectations along the way.

If you are starting your sustainability efforts from zero, or close to zero, it is very unlikely that you can develop a measurable long-term strategy in three months, even though it may be one of the first deliverables your sponsors ask you to develop. The risk is to aim too high ('we will double our widget production and sales, while at the same time halving all associated environmental impacts, and all within two years'). The other risk of course, is to aim too low ('all our employees will spend one day per year volunteering and switch off their PCs at the end of the working day'). There is too much you don't know right now.

Another frustration, and it is a frustration, is that where sustainability is concerned there are no elegant or template solutions for an organisation. Many leaders – and I experienced this at EDS – want certainty and clarity about what a strategy will deliver. I have worked with many clients who tell me they 'want a Plan A'. While imitation may be the highest form of flattery, taking what M&S has developed over a number of years (and through significant trial and error) does not guarantee success. There are too many variables, not only within the organisation itself, but its market and wider societal context.

It is realistic however, to begin to shape the vision of what your organisation can – maybe should – aspire to (think of this as True North), and how to develop the strategy. Don't lose sight of True North, even it can't be neatly quantified. In fact, some of the most courageous actions being undertaken by businesses in response to the challenges of sustainable development are being done in spite of an apparent lack of a more traditionally defined business case.

In the very short term, you probably need get some sense of where you are. Some of this information you will have already uncovered during your due diligence, or at least met the people who can help you track this down. You will also have an initial idea of the organisational context, which you will now need to supplement with a more external, market-led, analysis.

You might need to conduct some form of baseline or benchmark, but perhaps not within your first 100 days (such as energy consumption, carbon emissions, charitable donations, employee diversity, etc.), which will take time and quite possibly money.

The international framework ISO 26000 (**http://www.iso.org/iso/ discovering_iso_26000.pdf**) can be used at this stage as a prompt to what aspects of responsible business conduct may need to be included in your strategy. And, you will need to know what it is going to take in resource terms – time, people, and money – to make the strategy workable.

What resources do you have with the job, or is that something you need to define and negotiate for during this transition phase? Will these people be your direct team, or a matrixed team, bringing together resources from different parts of the organisation, none of whom are answerable to you? If you don't have a direct team, are you effective at building collaboration between virtual and multidisciplinary teams?

What is material to your organisation?

From the perspective of sustainability, one of the first areas to research is what is material to your organisation, that is to say, what social, environmental and economic factors does your organisation need to give attention to, because either they could harm (or benefit) your organisation or your stakeholders care about them?

Understanding materiality will help you get proportion, which in turn will allow you to focus resources on managing internal impacts that are significant for you during these early stages.

In 2008 EDS commissioned the Rocky Mountain Institute (RMI), to conduct a baseline of its environmental impacts prior to developing a sustainability strategy. As a global IT services business, with hundreds of office locations and service facilities (data centres, call centres, etc.) in more than 60 countries, this was a pretty significant and complex undertaking. RMI found that EDS's data centre operations accounted for 75% of the firm's total electricity use, and more than half of its global carbon footprint! From an environmental perspective it was resoundingly clear where the business needed to focus its efforts, and the resulting sustainability strategy focused on improving data centre efficiency.

EDS did not conduct a broader materiality analysis because the data (and EDS was a data-driven company, as I have mentioned before) identified what the business believed to be most material for the firm and also its stakeholders – namely electricity (consumption and cost) and other environmental factors (business travel, water, waste).

If you have worked at your organisation for a while, you may already have a sense of what is material for you, and ISO 26000 may help identify what it might be. Often the biggest determinant will be whether you 'make' stuff. EDS didn't manufacture, but it did 'host' millions – literally – of items of technology equipment from mainframes down to laptops. That is a lot of juice – and a mountain range of redundant kit to 'dispose' of.

What you may not have is any baseline data so that you can define the 'as is' state and therefore how the 'to be' will be different as a result of the programmes you will initiate and run. You need to include in your plan how you are going to get this baseline done, and how soon. How can you know for sure that you can reduce your electricity consumption by 30% in two years if you don't know what your consumption actually is and by what means (and with what investment and associated change management) it can be reduced? Depending on the size of your organisation, and its complexity, you may need external consultants to help you with this, as some of the data gathering is quite technical (and may require some impartial verification).

RMI calculated that EDS could reduce its greenhouse gas emissions by 33% over three years, with 75% of those reductions coming from energy optimisation in its data centre estate. I don't think anyone in the senior leadership team, let alone the operations managers who ran the data centres, would ever have believed that number without the evidence to back up the projections. And without that data, the EDS board would never have invested in the construction of an air-cooled data centre to host computing services for businesses and government departments. As it can cost several hundred million dollars to build an enterprise-scale 'mission critical' data centre, that is a huge commercial risk, especially when you are in the process of being acquired. But the board did approve, and the award-winning data centre opened for business in 2010.

There are lots of commercial consultancies out there, so good places to start in the UK are with the Carbon Trust (**http://www.carbontrust.com/ home**), Business in the Community (**http://www.bitc.org.uk**), or the ENDS Directory (**http://www.endsdirectory.com**) to give you some advice and connect you to the right people.

If you decide to conduct your own materiality analysis, you will need colleagues to help you do this and plenty of time. Section 4 in the linked document below, published by AccountAbility in 2006, outlines a comprehensive methodology for identifying and assessing material issues:

http://www.accountability.org/images/content/0/8/088/The%20 Materiality%20Report.pdf

What will all this give you? An evidence base, albeit subjective, and incomplete, of where you as sustainability lead need to focus the organisation's resources. For your risk-averse sponsors, it gives you the inputs for a mitigation plan. For sponsors who see sustainability as an opportunity, it highlights where potential for creativity and innovation might exist.

Take a look at the materiality analyses on the following organisation's websites; the visual representations and supporting commentary are very helpful (the presentation styles have been done for reporting purposes – there are a lot of input data that do not look so friendly):

Heinz: http://www.heinz.com/CSR2011/about/materiality_analysis.aspx

E.on: http://www.eon.com/en/sustainability/approach/stakeholder-management/materiality-analysis.html

PwC: http://www.pwc.co.uk/corporate-sustainability/materiality.jhtml

I have tried to simplify this as much as possible to give you a sense of how to make progress. But materiality is nuanced and has severe limitations. EDS, as a services-based organisation, faced significant commercial risk due to the rising costs of electricity. This had a bottom-line impact: rising operating costs for the business. It also had a top-line impact: to what extent EDS might be able to 'pass on' those increased costs and also prospective clients' procurement evaluation criteria where environmental responsibility had significant weighting (and competitors seemed to be scoring more highly).

Don't forget the golf balls

And then think about golf balls. Logo-branded golf balls. The kind of gifts that get handed out at trade fairs, open days, and used extensively when hosting client events.

One day, it turns out that the factory where those golf balls were made routinely employs children, has an appalling health and safety record and an international NGO picks up on the fact that your company has been buying golf balls made in this factory for years and no-one in your procurement team has ever assessed your supplier's (who is a corporate merchandise company) procurement standards. Your company is on the front page of the business section of the Sunday newspapers for condoning the use of children to make your branded goods. Twitter and Facebook are awash with angry posts and your PR department is in crisis-management mode and ignoring the journalists and escalating social media storm because no one can sign off an official position. And that big prospective customer, who was impressed with your environmental track record, and had just put you on a final supplier shortlist of one, reads about your lack of supplier due diligence. In a state of panic the sales team is on the phone to your CEO asking him to call the CEO of the prospective client, in the middle of the night if necessary, to give all the assurances under the sun that the matter is being dealt with and that it's really not an issue. Meanwhile, the guy in procurement, who has been buying these golf balls, tells you that he developed a supplier assessment and monitoring process years ago but his own leadership ignored it, because no one thought that low value goods, branded merchandise, presented any risk to the business.

This never happened to EDS, but when we debated what was material for the business, we often came back to the apparently inconsequential things that we couldn't quantify or track, and whether we had the capacity to try to tackle everything we could.

Pareto's Principle applies – focus your resources on where you can have the greatest impact. As I said before, what is material for your organisation may already be very clear. If it is, start there, because you can't tackle everything at once no matter how much you might want to. But remember that materiality is not measured in cost terms alone.

Oh, and one more curve ball. There is an old saying that what gets measured, gets managed. In the rush to quantify and mitigate your organisation's material impacts, it is entirely possible (and Carol Sanford, author of *The Responsible Business*, would argue inevitable) that you end up focusing on the wrong things to the detriment of the wider imperatives of a responsible business. Many of the greatest challenges society faces are external to the organisation and cannot be quantified (although there are people, such as TEEB, working on this). They are shared challenges that require shared responses.

Use the materiality as another input. But if there is something out there that makes you uncomfortable, in ways that you don't know how to articulate, let alone quantify, don't ignore it.

Your 30, 60, 90 day plan

Your 30, 60, 90 day plan should be a succinct summary of your transition. This document, and it may be easier to produce this in PowerPoint, should be high level but not generic. Start with the end in mind – what will you have done by the end of your first three months? What clarity is needed? How does that break down, month by month? How are you going to 'step up' over time?

Ideally, each section will have three to five main activities to support the key stages below:

30 **Finding out:** people and processes, roles, language, culture and resources. First draft of terms of reference. Go to meetings. Find your team and organisational allies.

60 **Testing:** start taking ownership of smaller projects, learn about bigger initiatives. Undertake initial materiality analysis and define resource needs.

90 **Ownership:** start taking a fuller leadership role. Deliver a high impact quick win. Sign off implementation plan for next phase.

My intention in this section was not to drown you in detail, but to highlight just how significant planning can be in preparing you to be successful; and for others to perceive you as effective. A significant part of this fact-finding is covered in the next section: understanding more about the market context.

2. Re-learn the organisational context

In your role as sustainability champion, you will have a perspective on your organisation that few outside of the leadership team have. Your remit may transcend functions, departments and geographies, bringing you into working contact with people you may never have encountered before no matter how long you have worked where you are.

Find someone, who isn't your sponsor or mentor, to be your tour guide. Who do you need to meet, and on what terms? Are there taboos and 'don't even go there' subject areas? If you are joining a new tier of management in your organisation you will be entering a domain of pre-existing relationships, shared history and cultural norms. You need to be sensitive to the allegiances and factions, but not to play one against the other.

Beginner's mind

In your first 100 days you have the opportunity to be the new person again. You have permission to reintroduce yourself to your peers and ask 'stupid' questions. You will have already undertaken some initial due diligence in your first 10 days, and now is the time to dig deeper and wider.

What is the wider context in which your organisation operates? What is already being done, perhaps under the radar, which can be leveraged? What perspectives, expectations and opinions exist about what sustainability means for your organisation? What do your customers, competitors and key opinion leaders say about you?

If you work for a commercial organisation, then a key driver for sustainability will be how you can use it to create a market advantage. Right now there are a few organisations that embrace sustainability solely because it is the right thing to do, without a supporting business case. And as important as it is to minimise harm – environmental, social, economic impacts and risk – an enduring and long-term strategy is one that also focuses on creating opportunities and a wider societal and environmental 'value'.

I worked with one organisation where there was an internal tension between the leadership as to whether or not they should focus on 'internal' matters (such as governance, green office, employee engagement) or manage what some saw as their biggest risk, which was their investment strategy. Having started in one direction (inside-out), a year later they decided to change direction (outside-in).

For organisations such as this, and maybe yours too, knowing where to start was a significant obstacle, and deciding to change direction was equally hard. Your role may be to help navigate that decision-making process.

From the planning stage, you may already have developed an initial view of what is material to your organisation. You may already have, or have commissioned, baseline data. Your first task here is to meet people, hear diverse views and sit in on meetings. As you move beyond the first 100 days, it will help you to frame those insights into organisational competencies, stakeholders and market analyses.

Surveying the landscape

There are many pre-existing tools and methodologies to help you gather these data. If you have a background in business management (or have an MBA, for example) you will know these and many others. Your organisation may have its own methodologies, or routinely survey the market.

Porter's Five Forces (**http://hbr.org/2008/01/the-five-competitive-forces-that-shape-strategy/ar/1**), for example, is a method of conducting industry (or market) level analysis with a view to determining how to create competitive advantage.

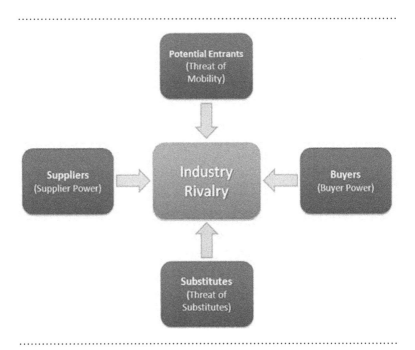

Political, Economic, Social, Technical, Legislative and Environmental (PESTLE) and Strengths, Weaknesses, Opportunities & Threats (SWOT) analyses (**http://www.businessballs.com/pestanalysisfreetemplate.htm**) can help you understand the market better, your organisation's place in it and how well equipped you are to respond.

Here is an example of a PESTLE analysis for a pharmaceutical company:

	Issue	Impact on business
Political	Global governments looking for healthcare savings	Increased pressure on pricing

Economic	Global economic crisis	Reluctance of consumers to spend on healthcare
Social	Increasing age of population and growth in obesity	Market likely to grow with increasing health concerns
Technological	Customised treatments	Direct to patient communications
Legislative	Increased litigation	Quality becomes key
Environmental	Growing environmental agenda and community awareness	Identify eco-opportunities to market

See this website for the full PESTLE analysis: http://www.strategic-planet.com/2011/01/a-pestle-analysis-for-the-pharmaceutical-industry/

The big global consultancies – such as PwC, KPMG, E&Y, Deloitte and Accenture – conduct frequent industry surveys. And there are smaller firms – such as Verdantix, SustainAbility, Trucost or Best Foot Forward – who undertake specialist work. Many of these organisations' findings are freely available. There are many consultancies out there; by naming a few I am not intending to exclude others.

Critically, involve others in this fact-finding and analysis, if for no other reason that you build consensus among your allies and the outputs are not one person's perspective.

Doesn't everyone feel the same?

I had been at EDS for eight years before I took on the sustainability role. In that time, I had worked in three parts of the business – sales, delivery and consultancy – and with colleagues across the globe. My network was pretty well developed and diverse, and through my network I had good access.

When I began to meet some of these colleagues again in my new capacity, I was unprepared for what happened. Not just once, but pretty consistently. As I met these people on a one-to-one basis, to explain my role and the sustainability ambition, and what I hoped to achieve, these managers said no to my requests for help. Not because they did not support or like me, nor because they didn't care on a personal level about sustainability, but because there was absolutely no benefit to them to say yes.

My assumption, and my error, was in thinking that integrating sustainability into business strategy was inherently right, and once it had been explained, others would agree and act, especially my supporters. It didn't work like that. Some of these colleagues told me what they needed me to do to help them, so that they could say yes. With one or two, I blew my opportunity and my credibility as a savvy operator by overdoing my enthusiasm.

Adding value

When you meet colleagues for the first time – either as completely new encounters or in your new capacity – focus on how you might help them. What are the big items that cause them pain? What problems do they need to solve? What do they need?

Over time, start to map out these relationships. Ideally, you want to shift your colleagues from adversaries and detractors to supporters and allies, or at least neutral.

Who are they?	What is the win-win?
Potential adversaries	
Detractors	
Neutral	
Supporters	

....

Partnering allies

_____   _____

_____   _____

_____   _____

....

Missing

_____   _____

_____   _____

_____   _____

....

Your early energy should be spent nurturing your allies and supporters. They become your advocates and implementers. As far as possible, if possible, don't try to convert people. You will be expending energy at the expense of those who can help you.

And as you prepare to meet these colleagues again, by way of a follow up, analyse the strategies available to meet the organisational and personal goals. Cover all the organisational functions:

Function	Concerns
Leadership team	• growth • market leadership • investor return • legacy

Legal	• compliance • governance • reporting • risk • ethics
HR	• motivation and engagement • recruitment & retention
Finance	• accounting for sustainability • investment • IRR
Marketing	• reputation • stakeholders • CSR • communication
Sales	• supplier credentials, • new client RFPs • referenceability
Operations	• OPEX • procurement (energy, etc.) • ICT & facilities management
Product/delivery	• product development • customer service • innovation
Who else...?	

Here is a simple tool to reframe what you hear during your first meetings into options that you can refer to when developing the strategy and as you become a resource for these colleagues.

TIPS: Trends, implications and possible strategies

Stakeholder view	Trends	Implications	Possible strategies
Meet as many people as you can, from as many parts of the organisation	What are the sustainability threats and opportunities that will affect us over the next 24 months?	What does it mean for us, what reactions are likely, how could or should we respond?	What tactical and strategic options are available to us to mitigate and create value?
Person A			
Person B			

The TIPS framework is useful because as you start to 'sell' the principles of sustainability within your organisation, this structure helps you to focus the discussion on the way forward and the options. It would be very easy to labour the 'FUD' factor (fear, uncertainty and doubt) associated with inaction and risk, but how many times have you heard the saying 'bring me solutions not problems'? TIPS helps you find the win-win solutions and takes you out of your own departmental or functional biases.

Don't limit your meetings to colleagues within your organisation. Make the time to meet, *and to listen to*, customers, business partners, suppliers and representatives from the local community.

3. **Achieve something**

You are going to have to deliver something during these first 100 days. It may be very apparent from day one what that 'thing' is, and it may be within your control to make it happen quickly. Does that mean you should go ahead and get it done by day two? Maybe. It is a sure way to show the impact you can have, to stimulate what can become a chain of change, and let's face it, it's hugely satisfying to get something done.

Conversely, if you do something that quickly, and apparently so easily, you set an expectation that you can repeat it, and if you can't, high praise might become criticism. And then you are dealing with a perception battle as well as a delivery challenge. You will know what's right when you decide what to do and when.

This section contains a few guiding principles to getting something done, and a tool for creating a near-term plan if you have an abundance of opportunities or aspirations to build on.

Deciding on the quick win

Make your sponsor look good – while we might wish it were otherwise, a tacit rule in getting stuff done at this stage is to make your sponsor look good. He or she needs the validation of knowing that it was a smart move to appoint you and that you will be a valuable resource. And you should benefit from the halo effect. What this deliverable is might be very clear and explicitly stated. If not, get some guidance.

Don't focus on your own hobbyhorse too soon – it is likely that before you even started the job, long before your 10 days of due diligence, you knew exactly what you wanted to do. Don't lose sight of that, but don't make it the first thing you do either. You need to earn the right, and there may be other more politically expedient things to address first.

Do something that is more than symbolic – in the rush to get something done, it might be easy to find fruit that is so low hanging it has bruises. There is a balance between delivery and symbolism. Do something that counts, and is achievable.

Don't make change for change's sake – it's an old adage, but if it ain't broke don't fix it. Closely aligned to symbolism, make sure that what you're about to change/deliver really needs to be done. It might take a while, and some research, to work that out.

Involve others – a lot of the content of this DōShort is about you as the change agent. However, everything you do will involve the involvement and consideration of others. Start to build those critical networks and ties by involving colleagues in what the early successes might be and genuinely celebrating the success as a team accomplishment.

Finally, quick wins are indicative of a short-term mindset. While it is important to have an early success, for all the reasons outlined above, that kind of thinking should not influence how you look at the bigger picture (back to True North). The most significant thing that you do may take years, with an uncertain payback, and a huge investment of resources, to make reality before you even see the impact. But what else can you keep in progress as you work towards that wild, hairy and audacious goal? **You need to plan for the short and the long term in parallel.**

Creating an action plan

When I was given the role of leading sustainability for EDS in EMEA, I had no idea of what to do and how to get started. As I spoke with colleagues – some from my network, others more recent relationships – the list of possibilities and priorities became longer. Some things were already in progress. EDS in the UK had already established a relationship with the Carbon Trust to undertake a preliminary environmental baseline. At a corporate level, EDS had begun to work with RMI on a global environmental strategy. These were significant, but also completely invisible to the majority of EDS's stakeholders. We had to do something that employees, and clients, could engage with in some way.

We were a core team of three plus around a dozen colleagues across the EMEA region. In the absence of a method of working out what we should do, and any direction or precedent, the core team defined its own process. Not only did this give us a structured plan of what to do, but the justification and rationale for the activities made sense to our sponsors.

The action plan became not just the means for delivering our quick wins, but the primary driver for the main implementation plan. Another team was working on EDS's global strategy, being led by the US, which we were also involved with, into which we would eventually have to integrate, but in the short to medium term we could do what was right for the EMEA region.

....

Step 1 **Brainstorm:** bring together a diverse group of colleagues, somewhere between six and 10, and brainstorm all the sustainability related activities that could or should be done. At this stage, no idea is too difficult to achieve or too small to be considered. Spend about 45 minutes doing this. Ideally, attendees should have had time before the session to reflect on this.

As a group, review the ideas (perhaps post-it notes on a wall, etc.) and remove duplicate ideas.

....

....

Step 2 **Identify impacts**: give an initial 'benefit' marking for
each idea. Use up to six possible impacts (for example,
environmental, community, cost, sales, governance, brand).
So, for example, one idea – removing waste paper baskets
from under every desk – might have environmental, cost
and employee impacts. Another idea – implementing
ISO140001 – might have environmental, governance, sales,
employee and cost impacts.

Create a long list of the ideas that have the most impacts.
You could, for example, select all the ideas that have at
least three positive impacts.

....

Step 3 **Ease of implementation**: from the long list, now classify the
ideas into how easy they might be to implement. For example,
Easy might be 'no senior-level approval or budget required,
immediate "payback"'. *Medium* might be 'senior approval
needed, process change, investment but with payback
within one year'. *Difficult* might be 'strategic board decision,
organisational implications and longer-term payback'.

Now group these ideas into clusters of ease. Do all the
people in the room have the resources and networks to
make some of these activities happen?

....

Step 4 **Building a plan**: create an implementation plan – with due
dates and responsibilities – of the activities you and your
team want to undertake. The timeline could be anything
from three months to three years. If three months, you will
probably want to focus on the tasks that you classified as
'easy' to implement. Identify the quick wins in the plan.
Indicate what the impacts are for each activity and how that
can be 'measured'.

....

Share the plan with your sponsor and other key supporters. Does the plan make sense politically as well as practically? What other resources might you need to deliver this plan?

Step 5   **Do and communicate**: deliver what is in the plan. Use the early successes (and challenges) as a communication tool for your employees and key stakeholders, too. In parallel, you will be working 'from the other direction' in terms of developing and validating the strategy. Do these activities complement the bigger vision? Does this plan need to be revised – deliverables, timelines, impacts?

How can you use these early wins and successes to engage more allies – champions – across the organisation?

Building a sustainability plan from the outputs of a brainstorm may not seem particularly rigorous or strategic. In the absence of a well-evidenced strategy, or the ability to make big things happen, you will have to start from somewhere. Why not start with what you and your colleagues know and have confidence can make happen?

In the experience of EDS, when we did this brainstorm most of the ideas we came up with were not trivial or symbolic. They were major changes – be it to a core business process or activity – that we could see would have measurable environmental, economic and brand impact, even if we didn't yet know how it could be measured.

At the time, back in 2008, there were not many resources (such as example plans) available to sustainability teams. Downloadable guides and plans for initiating sustainability initiatives are widely and freely available now. They are necessarily generic. What can set you and your team apart is your insight and understanding of the organisation. Use it to your advantage to create a plan that is tailored. The five-step process above may help you get that.

Brainstorms that buzz

Making a brainstorming session successful is hard work, and some academic researchers even doubt the usefulness of brainstorming as a method to solicit ideas and gain buy-in. I think brainstorming is valuable – when the session has been properly prepared, it is action-oriented and the participants get to see their contributions taken forward.

If you would like to top up your brainstorming toolkit, there are some unconventional resources out there. First, *Gamestorming* is a book and website (**http://www.gogamestorm.com**) that offers sets of creative practices for facilitating innovation.

The second is a Technology of Participation (ToP) methodology (developed by the Institute of Cultural Affairs) that is widely used by inter-governmental agencies, where consensus can be hard to reach! This downloadable guide from the University of Wisconsin-Madison is a great step-by-step guide to using the ToP tools:

http://oqi.wisc.edu/resourcelibrary/uploads/resources/Facilitator%20 Tool%20Kit.pdf

And this guide from the Asia Foundation is a comprehensive summary of the methodology:

http://asiafoundation.org/resources/pdfs/11TechnologyofParticipation TOP.pdf

These tools offer a contrast in approach, for you to adopt and adapt depending on the culture of your organisation.

Managing change

You are now a change manager of perhaps the most extensive and transformational change your organisation might undergo. If you have no experience of leading change, and even if you do, you could be overwhelmed as to how to go about it.

Think of your first 100 days as the initiation period of an organisational change programme. As you transition into the role, you will need to initiate a whole series of related activities, some foundational. Managing change is no insignificant task and there is a burgeoning market of consultants, interims and advisors who focus on it. Change and ambiguity is a common feature of many organisations, and in the global social, environmental and economic climate we find ourselves in right now, lots of things feel uncertain.

Perhaps the most well-known method is management guru John Kotter's 8-Step Change Model:

1. Establish a sense of urgency

2. Create the guiding coalition

3. Develop a vision and strategy

4. Communicate the change vision

5. Empower broad-based action

6. Generate short-term wins

7. Consolidate gains & produce more change

8. Anchor new approaches in the culture

If you want to know more about Kotter's model, see this *Harvard Business Review* article (you may need to register for full access): **http://hbr.org/2007/01/leading-change-why-transformation-efforts-fail/ar/1**.

There are many reasons why organisations are so resistant to change. You will need to be patient and persistent, accepting that you may achieve a percentage of all the change that you see as possible and necessary. Following a 'structured' approach to managing change gives you the means to learn as you go along, as well as providing others with the assurance that what is happening is not random (although some of the change that does happen will be more random, or emergent).

Be open to emergent change

During my time at EDS the organisation went through one of the most disruptive shocks imaginable to what was once the largest and most successful IT services company – it was acquired. Anxiety and uncertainty pervaded the business, all the way from individuals wondering whether they would still have a job (and many people did lose their jobs, and HP is still shedding staff today) to sales teams hoping that prospective clients (negotiating billion dollar deals) would take the risk and sign.

That is an extreme case of unplanned, market change. There is no way we could have influenced or controlled what happened to EDS! What we could do, and did do, however, was to re-evaluate our plan to see what we felt sure *could* happen, and to identify new opportunities that arose. This is one aspect of emergent change. As we integrated into HP, we found new allies and opportunities. But it did mean we had to let some things go because they became too hard to fight for.

Penny Walker (**http://penny-walker.co.uk**), environmentalist and facilitator, says that emergent change is the inevitable result of all the tiny conversations, actions and responses that go on every day in and around an organisation. And if we accept that transition towards sustainability cannot be achieved without changing beliefs, then emergent change must be a part of achieving sustainability.

So embrace emergent change, and adapt with it. It means change is happening and taking on its own momentum. What has shifted in the cultural norms of your organisation that presents you with allies? What else can you do with your resources now that project X has been put on hold? Who has been promoted, and how can you help them be successful? Which organisational cluster (team or group) is making the most progress?

As I said before managing change is a significant topic, and not the focus of this DōShort. A really practical workbook written for sustainability practitioners is Penny Walker's *Change Management for Sustainable Development*, which is available from the Institute of Environmental Management and Assessment's website (**http://www.iema.net/ publications/practitioner/8**). There are downloadable templates from this site, too.

4. Be resilient and adaptable

This final tool is all about you – and how you maintain balance and satisfaction through meaningful work. Like most of the other tools in this DōShort, this is not an activity to be completed in your first 100 days, but rather the beginning of what should become an ongoing process.

From having observed others take on the role of sustainability champion, and reflecting on my own experiences, I think there are three key shifts that need to occur in your mindset: recognition (how do people now perceive you), congruence (are you aligned to your values) and behaviours (interpersonal skills, influencing).

Finding meaning through work

Marjolein Lips-Wiersma, an expert in organisational behaviour, has spent many years studying meaningful work. Through her research, she has observed that there are four pathways to meaning (being, doing, self and others), but they have inherent tensions.

We need to find balance between our human need to focus inward and reflect, and our need to act in the world. And at the same time we face the ongoing challenge of meeting the needs of the self, while also meeting the needs of others. Meaning is found by working through all pathways, and in balancing or addressing their fundamental tensions.

A sustainability transformation, while it will impact the tangible and the measurable, as well as the intangible, will also require a far deeper engagement, asking questions about what it means to be responsible and to whom. These are questions that will require reflection and discussion.

If you want to know more about the Map of Meaning, including how you might use it for yourself and your team, to create shared goals and align values, see Marjolein Lips-Wiersma's website at **http://www. holisticdevelopment.org.nz/using-the-map/using-the-map**.

What's driving you?

Of course you want to make an impression, show progress and conquer the known universe. And if that means being on a call with a colleague from Australia at 6 am UK time, you'll do it. And if, on that same day, a senior manager in Silicon Valley can only speak to you at 9 pm UK time, you'll do it. And when your sponsor tells you – on a Friday – that he or she has a meeting with a key client on Monday and could you just prepare a couple of slides on key talking points, you'll do it. And if that means ignoring your spouse at breakfast time, or cancelling a long-held evening appointment, or spending the weekend in the study while the family is having a BBQ in the garden, well, that goes with the territory of senior responsibility doesn't it?

Pardon the pun, but that attitude is not sustainable. Pretty soon your first and last act of the day, every day, will be checking email. Your smartphone will go everywhere with you, and I mean everywhere. You will be living in your thoughts. Maybe your life is already like that.

We all have times when we have to drop everything to respond to an urgent need. That's life. And sometimes that does mean being on a conference call when you should be sleeping. It happens, especially if you work for a global organisation. There are negative consequences, however, aside from letting your friends and family down. You are raising your stress levels, increasing your risk of burnout and ultimately stifling your own creativity. So, by all means work hard, put in the hours and spin as many plates as you want to. And, at the same time, put as much effort into maintaining (or even finding) hobbies, down-time and being in the moment.

This is particularly hard when it comes to sustainability. Chances are, you are doing this role because of a personal drive to change your organisation, acting on your beliefs and putting your heart into the job. If you were volunteered to do this, you'll want to do it right. And when you're doing something you are so motivated about how can you just switch off, stop or say no?

Actually, I don't know. This is something I am not very good at. Over the years, I have jumped on a plane at half a day's notice to go on a two-week business trip, I have said yes to things even though I had no idea where I was going to find the time or energy, I have missed social events because something really needed to be done by the end of the day, and I have stopped going to the classes I signed up to after one or two sessions.

Where are your values?

What I have learned though, the hard way, is what a balanced life means to me. Front and centre, it means living my values and not leaving them at the door to where I work. I now have these values written down on a piece of paper, like my own Rosetta Stone, and every so often I look at them to remind myself before I say yes to the next thing. But it's a work in progress of making intentional choices and not just reacting (okay, I still react too, sometimes).

If this sentiment has resonated with you, you might enjoy this article on the *Harvard Business Review* website: **http://blogs.hbr.org/cs/2012/08/ the_disciplined_pursuit_of_less.html**.

Phil Bolton, a career coach who runs Less Ordinary Living (**http://www. lessordinaryliving.com**), says that clarifying and prioritising your values is an important step in designing career goals that will bring happiness and success. He outlines the following steps:

1. Identify 10 values that describe who you are and what is central to your being: these could be concepts (honesty), actions (spending time with family) or anything else that is important to you.

2. Take time to review the values and ensure that they are complete – make any changes you would like to.

3. Prioritise the values. Ask yourself which is more important: 1 or 2. Compare the more important with 3. Use this process to identify your top five values.

Now, how can you ensure those values are reflected in the choices you make at work and at home? Only you know what a balanced life will look like for you.

Peter Bolt, in his book *The Whole Manager – Achieve Success without Selling Your Soul*, suggests it is possible to succeed without sacrificing your integrity, your home life or your self-respect. It is a very practical and down-to-earth guide on 10 simple strategies to manage yourself more effectively, and well worth the read.

Making sustainability happen in an organisation is a marathon, not a sprint. It requires stamina more than speed. Train appropriately.

Adjusting to leadership

Whether you are in this job because you got 'promoted', or you are self-appointed, you are now an organisational leader. This doesn't necessarily mean that anyone is going to listen to you any more than they did before, or respect your position, but it does mean that perceptions and expectations will shift. Your first 100 days is your opportunity to develop the goodwill that you will need as you settle into the role.

So what kind of leader do you want to be? And what skills and resources do you need to become that person? And what is it about you that might get in the way?

How you decide to act is your call in response to the organisational and cultural context you find yourself in. One of the most significant problems with the first 100 days is the expectation – albeit unspoken – that you are going to get it right from day one: every decision expertly judged, every meeting a success, all the objectives on the plan achieved. It may not work out that way, however, not just because of our good friend emergent change, but also because you are learning as you go along.

Psychologists, building on a model developed by Noel Burch, say there are four stages of learning:

Unconscious incompetence → conscious incompetence → conscious competence → unconscious competence

When you don't know what you don't know, your anxiety levels are low. But when you realise what you don't know this increases your stress and decreases performance. Over time you become skilful until what you are doing feels like second nature and you don't even have to think about it.

So, while colleagues around you in your first 100 days may be expecting peak performance, be kind on yourself. You are getting there, even when it's bumpy and uncomfortable.

Throughout this DōShort I have alluded to a view that perhaps the most challenging (and when addressed, most profound) shift that is required within an organisation transitioning towards sustainability is around its beliefs and culture(s). Your role as leader is to help make this shift happen.

The following resources develop these ideas further:

Start with why: Simon Sinek 'argues that as individuals and companies, everything that we say and do is a symbol of who we are. And it is only when we communicate our beliefs authentically that we can attract others to our cause, and form the bonds that will empower us to achieve truly great things'. Watch his engaging talk here:

http://www.ted.com/talks/simon_sinek_how_great_leaders_inspire_action.html

Changing business from the inside out: 'Whether your worldview is that corporations are inherently selfish or are more prone to act in the public's interest, it is undeniable that the free-market economy is the dominant social institution of our time.' See the excerpt (and book) by Tim Mohin on socially responsible business:

http://www.huffingtonpost.com/tim-mohin/occupy-from-the-inside_b_1199104.html

Building your support network

One of the most common experiences of sustainability champions is isolation. You are entering into a role that is most likely new to that organisation, ill-defined in the market and with competing and contradictory demands. You may not have a team or budget, even though you have had significant responsibility in other roles. You may sit in an organisational vacuum, with the remit of a senior manager but the authority of a middle manager. You are transitioning into a new role, and possibly also a new working identity, even if you have your former colleagues and networks around you.

To help you manage your own development, and to keep a sense of perspective, it may be helpful to find a coach or mentor. It could be a colleague within the organisation – but not your sponsor – or an external resource.

There are other benefits of coaching that extend beyond your own performance. Article 13, a sustainability consultancy, say that the nurturing of a coaching culture within teams and organisations is highly complementary to a focus on sustainability. This is because coaching encourages an orientation towards positivity, development, increasing awareness and responsibility, and focus on impact in the real world (**http:// www.article13.com/csr/sustainability_coaching.asp**). As you learn the skills and benefits of coaching, you can bring that mindset to your teams.

Once you start to undertake activities within your organisation, it is very likely that others will show an interest and want to get involved in some way. These early allies are invaluable to you, not just in terms of finding an internal network of like-minded colleagues, but perhaps more importantly they can become your 'champions', with whom you can communicate via the informal networks, share tasks and generate ideas.

You can also look beyond your organisation for support. Online networks and communities that have useful content, participants and tools include (some of these are free to join):

- Association of Sustainability Practitioners
  http://www.asp-online.org

- Global Association of Corporate Sustainability Officers
  http://www.gacso.org

- Guardian Sustainable Business Network
  http://www.guardian.co.uk/sustainable-business

- International Society of Sustainability Professionals
  http://www.sustainabilityprofessionals.org

- Two Degrees Network
  http://www.2degreesnetwork.com

There are also one- or two-tiered membership organisations, including:

- Institute of Environmental Management and Assessment
  http://www.iema.net, which has an environmental bias but is
  now broadening its focus and reach.

- Society for the Environment
  http://www.socenv.org.uk/cenv/

And, if you like the idea of meeting real people, there are social and peer
networking organisations. The two best known are:

- Green Drinks http://www.greendrinks.org, a global, self-
  organising informal community that brings together all people
  with an interest in sustainability, and

- Green Mondays http://www.greenmondays.com, a UK, mainly
  London-based, business network with more structured access,
  format and content.

Finally, LinkedIn (as well as Facebook and Twitter, for that matter) has hundreds of sustainability-related groups, covering all impact areas, industries and geographic markets. Search on the word 'sustainability' in these applications and see what takes your interest.

Unlike many other organisational challenges, sustainability as an issue and management approach has come of age at the same time as the development of the Internet. The downside is a potential deluge of information, not all of it created equally. The upside though, is access to people, ideas and information, whenever you need it, which is constantly changing as new developments take place.

....

But What About Sustainability?

THE INTRACTABLE SUSTAINABLE development challenges of climate change, renewable energy, resource scarcity, water, well-being and prosperity, the rising middle class in fast developing economies, the poor at the 'base of the pyramid', consumerism and consumption, are no longer subjects for discussion solely by environmentalists and 'tree huggers'. They affect your organisation and its entire value chain.

Sustainability, when properly integrated into the businesses strategy and goals, has the potential to affect change in every department, function, team, location, and stakeholder – all the way from the smallholder supplier to the CEO.

That's a massive transformational undertaking that won't happen in the short to medium term and will require iterations, a positively engaged leadership team and significantly more time and effort than you want it to take. To that extent, the success of you as the sustainability champion will most likely be less about your 'technical' sustainability knowledge – at the micro-level – and more about your ability to integrate, join dots, build coalitions, manage ambiguity and influence. All the things we have been talking about above.

Professor Dexter Dunphy, from the University of Technology, in Australia, outlines in his book *Organizational Change for Corporate Sustainability* the six phases that all organisations can go through: Rejection, Non-Responsiveness, Compliance, Efficiency, Strategic Proactivity and finally the Sustaining Corporation. Most businesses, he says, start their transition to incorporating sustainability into the business once they enter the compliance phase.

It would help you, and also help set expectations, to know where you are on this curve. Can you make more happen than your organisation is ready for? Can you leapfrog straight to a Sustaining Corporation (probably not)? And also where has the organisation aspirations to be, and over what duration?

Am I saying you don't need to 'know' anything about sustainability? Of course not! You'll need to know a significant amount – what the impacts, threats and opportunities are for your industry, organisation, supply chain, customer base, as well as the nuances for each part of your organisation. You'll need to know how to translate that into strategic business risk for senior leadership, to capture the hearts and minds of employees and customers, to incentivise innovation (whether that's fixing a broken process or inventing a new product) and to know when to leave a closed door closed.

Whether you want to complement that knowledge with grounding in environmental management or social accounting, for example, may very well be dependent on your own aptitude for learning, organisational culture and the roles you have had previously (you might even have a technical past in health & safety or negotiating land rights with indigenous communities).

What you need to know will be highly contextual, but for a good generic entry into this world you could start here:

Business in the Community's business case for sustainability: http://www.bitc.org.uk/media_centre/comment/the_future_of.html

Adam Werbach on when sustainability means more than green:
http://www.mckinseyquarterly.com/When_sustainabillity_means_
more_than_green_2404

Much wisdom and research has gone into the evolution of what sustainability means. Perhaps the most accessible historical digest is *The Top 50 Sustainability Books*, published by Greenleaf in partnership with Cambridge University's Programme for Sustainability Leadership: **http://www.green leaf-publishing.com/add_getquantity.kmod?productid=2930**. As the title suggests, the book provides summaries and perspectives on the 50 most influential books and authors who have informed the environmental and social debate. It's worth dipping into if you have the time.

From 100 to 1000 Days, and Beyond

HERE WE ARE AT DAY 101. Did some big page turn, like in children's stories? The goal of this DōShort was to prepare you for an effective transition in your first 100 days, to share what I think are the most valuable tools, planning being top of that list, so that as you move into days 101 to 1000, and even beyond, you are building on solid foundations.

But what *does* happen next? The short answer is that the ongoing programme will be built from a number of sources – what your sponsors want, what you are required to do, what you have the courage to try, what your stakeholders expect you to do and how you respond to emergent change and market shifts. No two sustainability programmes are alike, nor should they be, because every organisation's context is unique. So what happens next is down to you and your team.

But there will be some common considerations:

- The rationale for change (why, exactly?).

- Knowing who the ultimate beneficiary is (wider society, the value chain, the organisation) and whether are they being positively impacted.

- What the social, ethical, environmental and economic factors are and how they are to be measured and managed (risks and opportunities).

- Defining and implementing practical work streams of activity.

- How to integrate sustainability into the organisation 'sustainably'.

- Measurable financial, environmental and social impacts.

- Who the stakeholders are and how they want to be engaged.

- What and how to report, to whom and to what standards.

- Doing things differently, perhaps even stopping some stuff altogether.

- Motivating (and incentivising) others to act, facing resistance and indifference.

- Telling your story, to employees, customers and others.

- Governance and assurance, whether legislated or voluntary.

- Dealing with criticism, failure and adverse attention (it happens).

- Ambiguity and contradictions (can you have prosperity without growth?).

- Responding to externalities (climate change, consumption and its impacts).

- Advocacy (be it policy, legislation, employee, NGO or peer pressure).

- Getting recognition for what's been achieved.

- Raising the bar of performance and aspiration.

- Making sure that sustainability doesn't become a departmental ghetto that no-one else in the organisation needs to engage with.

In my experience, what happens next is very much dependent on the buy-in and engagement of your organisation's leadership team. No-one is going to get in your way if you are leading projects that save money, promote efficiency and help win new business. But what if your ask is significantly greater than that? What if your ask comes with uncertainty, and a level of ambiguity?

I don't believe that this level of transformational shift comes from the middle of the organisation, or from the grassroots. Right the way through the first 100 days, and into the next 1000, you need your leadership team to lead. They need to set the agenda for change, even if you were the one who did all the working out.

If you are on the leadership team of your organisation, drive the change. If you report to someone on the leadership team, help shift his or her mindset. Be careful not to be seen as a marginal voice, or ghetto, in what is fundamentally changing the rules of the game for business. And then harness the passion and enthusiasm of your employees, your business partners, customers, suppliers, and the wider stakeholder community who know who you are even if you don't know them.

How many organisations have been 'doing' sustainability for long enough to be at a leadership stage? Arguably, very few. Joel Makower, thought leader and writer, says that there has been only one individual and organisation so far: Ray Anderson and Interface Inc. (a modular carpet company).

See Ray's quietly inspirational TED talk here: http://www.ted.com/ talks/ray_anderson_on_the_business_logic_of_sustainability.html

Final Thoughts

ONCE UPON A TIME, even Ray Anderson faced his first 100 days.

It might not feel like it right now, but in taking on the role of change agent, whether self-appointed, volunteered or 'promoted', you have done something courageous as well as downright scary!

You bring to this role all that you have learned and achieved to date, an openness to leap into the unknown and possibly a deeply held perspective about what organisational responsibility means in the 21st century. You can and will achieve your goals. You will achieve things you didn't set out to achieve. You will have to let some things go. And you will make mistakes.

The context of the change you will lead is unique to you, because every organisation is a unique mix of tangible and intangible facets. And the programme you create will be a reflection not just of the organisational context, but the lens though which you view it and how you make change happen.

In the absence of complete and perfect information you will be expected to lead and to act anyway. It is the *timing* of decision-making rather than the decisions per se that will set you apart. Harvard Business School academics Bob Eccles and Nitin Nohria call this 'robust action', which 'accomplishes short-term objectives while preserving long-term flexibility'.

You need to act in parallel with the development of a longer-term strategy, and with large doses of uncertainty, and in the context of an organisation that will be constantly shifting in response to internal and external stimuli.

You need to act.

You need to listen and lead.

You need to have a sense of True North and get the small stuff right.

I'll sign off with these words by Paul Hawken, environmental campaigner and entrepreneur, and the man who inspired Ray Anderson to transform Interface, at the Commencement Address to the Class of 2009, University of Portland:

> *You join a multitude of caring people. No one knows how many groups and organizations are working on the most salient issues of our day: climate change, poverty, deforestation, peace, water, hunger, conservation, human rights, and more. This is the largest movement the world has ever seen. Rather than control, it seeks connection. Rather than dominance, it strives to disperse concentrations of power. Like Mercy Corps, it works behind the scenes and gets the job done. Large as it is, no one knows the true size of this movement.*

As overwhelmed as you might feel in your first 100 days, there are millions of us out there making change happen. We're all working it out too. Welcome.

....

For Product Safety Concerns and Information please contact our EU
representative GPSR@taylorandfrancis.com
Taylor & Francis Verlag GmbH, Kaufingerstraße 24, 80331 München, Germany